BUILD YOUR IDEA IN 7 DAYS

A CRASH COURSE FOR TURNING YOUR IDEAS INTO REALITY

Jet Ellison

I0467795

<u>COMPLIMENTARY BONUSES</u>

Thank you in advance for reading this book.

To make sure you get the most value out of this book, here are three exclusive resources that will help you on your entrepreneurial quest.

1. "100 Ways to Gain More Time, Money and Happiness".

We compiled 100 ways to help spark more ideas on how to gain more money, time, and happiness. It is a must read companion with this book.

2. "45 Ways to Increase Productivity for the Entrepreneur"

This gives you 45 amazing ways to get yourself motivated to achieve greater levels as an entrepreneur or employee. Give it a quick read and apply it to your life.

3. "100 Amazing Tips to be a More Successful Entrepreneur"

This short book gives you 100 tips and tactics on becoming a better entrepreneur. Print it out and keep it by your side when you are in need of motivation.

You can download these three incredible resources here for free:

www.jetellison.com/amazongifts

Any questions, please don't hesitate to contact me at www.jetellison.com. If you'd like to connect with me on Twitter, follow @ellison_jet.

With gratitude,

Jet Ellison

FIVE STAR REVIEWS FROM FIRST EDITION

"This book gave me many ideas for my idea, hence the title. The book basically helps you work your way through your idea. It encourages you to start and make a change. It doesn't have to be a drastic change, just a small change. You can start with your environment or even which hand you wear your watch on as one of the points in the book suggests. These small things we think of may seem insignificant, but they help change our neural pathways."

- N. Stark

I especially love the end of each chapter where there are steps to take. I found some very enjoyable. This short book helps turn your idea into reality.

- Amazon Customer

I found this book to be engaging and helpful. The advice on Day 2 was enlightening in that I hadn't thought such simple changes in my surroundings could spark creativity. As an online business owner, the steps on Day 6 mirrored my experiences and also gave me ideas on how to do some different things as far as marketing. I really liked the blue box at the end of every "day" or chapter that summed up the information. It's a great book and a nice little read!

- Amazon Customer

This book lays out the plan for making an idea work. I think it is well written and the author offers his help by giving the reader his email. There are good websites and links in the book. I felt the book was worth reading!

- Amazon Customer

DISCLAIMER

Many hours from many helpers (proofreaders, editors, designers, friends, kindle book formatters) has gone into making this little book a resource that provides value to you, the reader. The aim is to reopen your creative mind and show you a way to act on your ideas. This book is designed for you and I hope you like it enough to leave a five-star review (although, any review at all would be lovely to receive!). Illustrations and designs by Riz Marie. For design inquiries, contact at rizzasimando[at]gmail.com.

Special thanks to all who helped contribute directly and indirectly to the publication of this book. Enjoy.

<u>WHO AM I?</u>

My name is Jet and I have been in technology businesses and start-ups for over a decade. I'm an avid traveller, however, my home is based in beautiful Sydney, Australia. My educational attainment (although much more has been learnt in the 'real world') is a Bachelor of Business, Masters of Business leadership and final stages of an Executive MBA.

This book began as a simple workable solution for family and friends. The objective now is that you find the same value within these pages. If you would like to contact me, please get in touch at JetEllison.com.

CONTENTS

INTRODUCTION

"If you haven't found it yet, keep looking. Don't settle. As with all matters of the heart, you'll know when you find it. And, like any great relationship, it just gets better and better as the years roll on."

- Steve Jobs, Founder of Apple

Are you seeking your own successful start-up?

Do you struggle to wonder which idea of yours to work on?

Do you have too many ideas or not enough ideas?

If you suffer from any of these scenarios, this course is for you. I say 'course', as this book is written to be applied over a week. It's an "idea development" course designed just for (excuse the corny acronym), EWE: Entrepreneur, Wanna-be-prenuer, Employee-preneur. It is about you, about developing your idea, and turning it into your reality.

We can all find answers quicker than we can finish the questions, and this access to information has successfully (or unsuccessfully) attributed to a decrease in our attention span - to shorter than a goldfish - according to recent studies. This book was designed to be read in seven days for you to digest small amounts of information at a time. If you can, avoid the natural inclination to skim the information here, try and entertain stretching and digesting this information over the next seven days, as that is how it has been written. Will you do that? Great! Now let's continue...

This is an innovative seven-day course that will look at using mindset, life hacks, tech hacks and idea development, specifically designed to make your idea generation, *'fun work'* (which doesn't have be an oxymoron!). Let's aim at getting the momentum flowing and help you find what will make you jump out of bed in the morning.

If you've come this far where you're thinking about your ideas to the point of downloading this book, maybe you are willing to come a little further and share the next seven days with me.

DAY ZERO: DECLUTTER YOUR LIFE.

"I'd be unstoppable if I just got started."

\- Unknown

In 2016, a Princeton University study looked at an individual's task performance in an organised and disorganised environment. The study found that excessive "stuff" in disorganised environments (your physical 'stuff') has a severe negative impact on your ability to focus and process any information. It therefore adversely affects your ability to create new ideas. If clutter in our physical space affects our performance, imagine what mental clutter in our mind's space is doing to us!

Forget the maxim that a clean house is a boring mind. If anything, it means you have more mental space to think clearly. Disorganised environments have been shown to negatively affect your performance, however, what is more important is how you perceive your personal clutter. Your perception of it is what really matters, not someone else's. If having a pen, photo, and notebook on your desk doesn't feel like it is disorganised, then it's not. But if you inherently know that those old newspapers on your desk aren't really ever going to be touched, then bin them.

You might be wondering what a messy environment has to do with idea creation and building your business. The truth is that it has everything to do with it. New ideas will only come in if they can see a home that's welcoming and inviting. Ideas need action and actions take time. So take the time to get these actions in order so new ideas have mental space to arrive and thrive.

This book isn't about getting your personal management system in order, so we won't take a deep dive down the never ending rabbit hole on this one. If you have a few days to spare, I would strongly suggest you read David Allen's 'Getting Things Done'. If you don't, here's a quick practical summary:

There are five steps for getting your life on track to leave room for more.

1. Process everything in your environment

Go through all your computer files and put anything you haven't touched for more than one month into a folder called 'Archive'. If something needs to be actioned, put it into a folder called 'Next Action'. Do the same with your email and anything that doesn't need an action, move it to your Archive email folder. If an action is required, create a 'Next Action' email folder.

Do the same with your physical environment. Clean your home from top to bottom and put things where they belong. Anything that needs actioning goes into a physical tray called an 'inbox'. You'll come back to this later. Don't forget your office, car, and garage. If you're like most people, this will take you a few hours. If it will take more, consider spending an upcoming weekend to process everything in your environment and read David Allen's book in the meantime. This process alone will be worth it.

By doing this, you'll not only find a few lost ideas (and other lost items) but also, some space available in your mind to move on.

2. Store all your information of what needs to be done in a system.

It's a great start to have an external physical 'inbox' and a couple of folders on your computer and emails for 'next actions'. Apart from the classic pen/paper scenario, consider using a good cloud-based software like Evernote, Todoist, or Trello. I personally use Trello as the Getting Things Done ("GTD") principles work seamlessly with it. If you are interested in understanding how to use Trello to maximise your ability in 'getting things done', check out Trello GTD Mastery. If you're interested in using Evernote, there are countless Evernote GTD books and forums for this combination. Whatever your system might be, check the resources section of this book, for a list of software and ideas to use with it.

3. Create time-lined lists for actioning item.

Once you've chosen your system, write down ALL the unclosed loops in your head and anything you ever want to do in your life (these are also unclosed loops). Write down everything from personal goals to professional goals, from small goals to big hairy audacious goals, from the mundane to the madness. Anything and everything needs a home, so jot it down or add it to your organisation tool.

4. The process by time constraints and use it religiously.

The next step is to give each of these items a time constraint. In Trello and Evernote, you can create different lists or sections to include these items. Personally, my task board includes the following lists; Someday/Maybe, Year, Quarter, Month, This Week, Next Action, References.

All of these should speak for themselves, except the last two. Next Item is the list of 'Next Action' tasks that you need to work on. You can also call this 'today', but it might not be 'today' that you get to it and the connotations associated with 'Next Action' give it a disciplined approach.

'Reference' is a great list to have where you can keep items you may need to look at on a recurring basis or that you know you want to remember. It's not for old receipts, although you can create a system or board for these such things. In my reference list, I have cards that are especially for 'Nonprofit Ideas', 'Travel Tech Ideas', and 'Billion-dollar Baby Ideas'. You could also have cards like 'Names to remember', 'Restaurants to try', and 'Birthdays to know'. You can pretty much have anything here that you think you may need to remember quickly.

After you have this setup (for additional help, see resource section), go through every item and give it a home on your system by allocating it a date range. Once you've finished your brain dump list, get to work and add any tasks from your physical 'inbox', as well as what is on your computer's 'next action' folder and 'email' next action folder.

5. Your own plan: The importance of a personal productivity system.

There is only a finite amount of time and a limited window of opportunity for most viable ideas, so you need to ensure you are prioritizing what matters most. This is where the importance of 'next action' items come into play. For any entrepreneurial endeavour, you will need a lot more mental capacity than you first thought!

If you don't have a personal productivity system, chances are you'll have more of a cluttered mind than most and you're doing yourself a major disservice. Just to up the Princeton researchers, Yale recently conducted a study that found the same areas of the brain fired when looking at 'clutter' as the areas which are associated with pain. The anterior cingulate cortex and insula, light up in response to letting go of items you own and feel a connection toward. This is the same part of the brain that lights up when you feel physical pain from a paper cut or drinking coffee that's far too hot. Your brain views the loss of one of your valued possessions as the same as something that causes you physical pain. And the more you are committed emotionally or financially to your clutter, the more you want to keep them around.

DAY ZERO SUMMARY

Forget new ideas until you get rid of your old actions. Do a 'brain dump' and purge as much stuff, both physically and mentally, as possible.

DAY ONE: HOW TO DEVELOP NEW IDEAS

"New ideas pass through three periods: it can't be done; it probably can be done, but it's not worth doing; I knew it was a good idea all along."

- Arthur C. Clarke, Writer

Let's get down to business.

Let's start this chapter with an old-fashioned pen and paper. For unknown reasons, creative thinking works better when it's in your own writing and not through a computer. For now, though, just trust me and use a pen and paper.

Write down all your ideas that you think are worthy. Have you written them all out? There is always some more so see what else you can think of. Great.

Is there one idea, perhaps you already know it, that you really want to work on? What you want is an incredible idea, an idea that will make you leap out of bed early in the morning.

If you didn't write any idea that comes even close, then you'll need to change your thinking to change the ideas you create. To get those 'eureka' moments you occasionally read about, you need to see every*thing* from a different perspective. View *things* through eyes that ask 'How can it be improved?' or 'Imagine if it could...' For most creative undertakings and 'ah-ha' moments, they were often either improved on or stolen from a past moment in history.

You've probably heard the quote "The idea just hit me out of thin air." That sounds great, and in some cases, ideas do seamlessly transpire out of thin air, however, that has only happened because your brain has joined the dots between whatever new information entered it and old information that was there before. If you aren't getting many new ideas, you are feeding it too much 'old' information. You need to increase new information so ideas can be developed and grow.

The key to that one lightbulb idea for you is to come up with *many* ideas. Yes, to get that one idea, you need *many* ideas. Ideas beget more ideas. This power can be found in an old-fashioned brainstorming session.

Brainstorming has only one rule: never prejudge an idea no matter how ridiculous or impractical, as it may lead to less ridiculous and more practical ideas. Whether you do it alone or with others, the key to a good brainstorming session is to just let the ideas flow: good, bad, and the ugly.

If you're stuck at some point, one of the most creative ways of getting out of the rut is to consciously try and connect two unrelated areas of interest. Lightbulb moments generally happen because your brain is unconsciously forming these neuropathways, however, it also works the same if you give it a helping hand and do this consciously.

A personal example is that I am a vegetarian and a novice bodybuilder. Bodybuilding and fitness aren't exactly synonymous with vegetarianism, so I created a plant-based fitness website that sells products for the 'plant strong' niche. Let us use another example. Say your hobbies are sewing fabrics and riding horses. Both are decidedly unrelated, but by linking sewing and horses, you may find some an innovative product or service. This is how "compression wear" for competitive horses were born.

What are two different interests of yours? Can you link your interests into a new idea?

Never judge the limitations of simple brainstorming. Someone might find the missing thread in what you may consider a crazy idea. Once the ideas are flowing, you'll want to milk it for as long as you can. If you're doing it by yourself, call up a friend and get their opinion. When you're finished you might not know exactly where to start narrowing them down, this can be an art unto itself. We'll address this issue later in the week.

Think about growing a hobby?

Believe it or not, some of the greatest businesses started out as little hobbies built on the intense passion of the founder. They have taken their love or enjoyment for something and turned it into a revenue-generating machine.

An example that comes to mind is Sean Plott. Sean Plott hosts an Internet TV show about a video game. He turned his hobby into a full-time job. The best part of it is that he actually enjoys what he is doing. He loves video games and now spends his days getting paid to talk about them. For him, life doesn't get any better than that, and he will continue that way, until he has had enough of video games.

Here's a handful of others who built empires from their passion;

1. Gary Vaynerchuk, a best-selling author and investor, started his empire by making wine videos.

2. The story goes that Mark Zuckerberg started Facebook to 'connect' with girls easier. That's a big passion for most 20 something-year-olds!

3. Brandon Stanton is a self-taught photographer who ended his bond trading career in 2010 to pursue his hobby as a photographer. Less than five years later his blog and books called "Humans of New York" have been massively successful all around the globe.

Building a business based on your hobby puts you at a massive advantage. Personally, I believe there is a special kind of unseen power in following your passion as you already have built-in motivation, knowledge, and mojo for it.

Take my word for it: running a business you have no interest in is extraordinarily difficult and it is a sure-fire way to get disheartened and fizzle out your momentum.

So, what are some of your interests? Is there any way that you could turn them into a business? There are many low-cost ways to test the water, from consulting and networking, to blogs and websites, stores and shows, videos and podcasts, and so on.

What have you always dreamed of doing?

Another place to look for great business ideas is in the things you have always dreamed of doing but never had a chance to do. If you've dreamed of it, why not build a business around that dream?

A quick disclaimer before we move on. The caveat in all this, of course, is to use your common sense. It's easy to say in words, harder in practice. As Chris Guillebeau says in his book the $100 Startup: "Good businesses provide solutions to problems". If your hobby doesn't pose a solution to a problem, then you better pass on it. Not everyone's passion or hobby is worth building, and not everyone wants their hobby to be their business. So again, use your common sense. To avoid getting caught up with ideas you don't really like, get smart with your choices to give yourself a better chance of success in business.

ACTION POINTS

To get new ideas flowing, let's aim at focusing on two things that will help you attain the right idea!

1) Read each day.

Find five minutes to read one short chapter a day for seven days.

If you can't find five minutes of uninterrupted reading, either wait until another week where you can dedicate yourself to the tasks at hand, or simply be creative and find a way (e.g. read it on your Smartphone on a toilet break or on a commute – pick up the audio version and listen to it while you work).

2) Do the five-minute *imprint* below.

These five-minute 'imprints' are mental exercises designed to improve your motivation and keep you disciplined as you move through the program. The desired effects of these changes show results in minutes, not months.

There has been much research into the 'quick change' field in the last decade. Psychologist professor, Richard Wiseman, author of 59 Seconds (a book devoted to research-based change strategies) believes that targeted short (and quirky) exercises will imprint you with a strong, enduring mentality.

The 5 Minute *Imprint* Action Steps

These two simple exercises are guaranteed to get your creative juices flowing:

1) Have a mini-brainstorming session with just yourself.

Grab a piece of paper (or open up a text document) and come up with 15 random ideas based on your interests, hobbies, or passions. Be varied, think of different things to associate. When you're done, rank them by what you think would be most successful. Give it some thought and then eliminate the bad ones and repeat until you end up with 15 great ideas.

2) Relating the unrelated.

The goal here is to pick two unrelated items from your personal interests and try to link them in a radically new way.

The next step. Tomorrow, you begin with Day Two which will set you down the path that will get you to your ideal business. It will come sooner than you think!

DAY 2: CHANGE YOUR SURROUNDINGS

"Life is like a dogsled team. If you aren't the lead dog, the scenery never changes."

- Lewis Grizzard, Writer

One of the best-hidden secrets of idea development is that making seemingly insignificant changes in your life, can spark new creativity.

When you switch, swap, and scramble your routine, your brain is forced to look at familiar situations in new ways, helping to create new neural pathways. The theory is that since we're forcing ourselves to be open to constant change, continual creativity is accessible in other ways. One of the abilities of the human condition is we get to our current circumstances. We get comfortable in our current environment and lifestyle, which is why change does such good things for our mind.

Now, before you upheave your whole life, know that small rapid changes can have the same long-lasting effects. In fact, this is our key objective: small changes for maximum results. What you need is the "MED", the Minimum Effective Dosage.

So let's focus on changes that won't take up too much of your time. Changing your computer background and display settings, listening to a radically different music genre, or picking up your laptop and moving to a new workspace can take mere seconds, and this is the kind of change, I advocate. This type of change will take less time or effort, and will still generate results.

Here are five environmental changes you can do immediately.

1. Hack your computer.

   Change your computer's background to something that represents the idea you want to grow. If you use Windows, move the horizontal bar to a different side. If your background settings allow, create a folder with a slideshow that you can use as your background. Change your icons, font colours. Create a subliminal message burner. Remember your subconscious is always working. For the more radically inclined, consider changing your QWERTY keyboard layout to Dvorak. It's arguably 38% faster than your current keyboard layout, however, the opportunity cost of switching will mean you will be slower in the short run.

2. Change your home page.

   Make your homepage an idea generation site such as entrepreneur.com or www.sethgodin.com. Better yet, consider making your homepage something you would never likely visit in a million years. Maybe it's the Barbie homepage or fruitarian's official homepage or a pro-communist website. Another great idea is to download a chrome extension called 'Momentum' which reminds you what your priority is each day.

3. Mobile apps.

   Download mobile applications related to your idea and delete Angry Birds and other anti-productivity apps! Go out of your way to find apps that will help develop your idea.

4. Information relevancy.

   Start listening to some idea generation podcasts (i.e. The Lifestyle Business Podcast, The Harvard Business Review, The Accidental Creative, The Smart People Podcast or Smart Passive Income) and find yourself some audiobook classics to help develop these ideas (a great recommendation is the late Jim Rohn or Earl Nightingale).

5. Avoid unnecessary information.

   Consider adopting a low-information diet on your kindle, phone, and computer. Hide all commonly accessible reading materials in your house that are not related to your idea. You want to focus only on what matters this week. Now buy three magazines, two related to the idea you have, and one on entrepreneurship or small business development. If you are on a shoestring budget, hit your local library.

Some people go so far as to make major sweeping changes all at once. Rarely does this last. While this can be mentally refreshing, it is a better strategy to do what seems like insignificant changes that you'll keep up with daily.

So what's the difference between making simple changes versus altering actions? While making small changes in your environment is great, you can take this one step further by beginning to do different things each and every day.

You can start off small, such as figuring out a new way to drive to work, start talking to new people or trying completely new activities outside your comfort zone.

By doing something like picking a new route to work, it will force you to consider something different than what you'd already long ago optimized and put on autopilot. Obviously, you don't want to make a million changes to your routine at once because that's overwhelming. It's better to ease the occasional change in.

The advantage to these constant changes is more than just creativity. It's keeping your mind sharp. For many of us, we simply become too comfortable in our methods. Whether you get married, launch a company, or fall in love, you will eventually get comfortable which is why change is so important to keep things afresh. By constantly adapting to change, you'll be primed and ready for when change does come around – good or bad.

ACTION IMPRINT STEPS

Figure out five small environmental things you can change this week (and keep it changed for a minimum of 21 days). Try to interject as much natural newness into your life as possible but don't try too many major changes at once.

The aim is to get you thinking differently and get you out of your comfort zone to infuse new information and creativity into your life so it's part of your consciousness. Consider implementing five small changes over the course of the next five days.

If you can't think of five, here are ten small changes you could choose from:

1. Wear your watch or jewellery on the other hand. When you start checking your wrong hand for the time, you'll realize how conditioned we really are and how important rewiring the brain is (please try this one, if only for a month; it is such a simple change with noticeable rewiring).

2. Start every morning with an audio book or podcast instead of the TV. If it's the right podcast, you'll get more laughs and find yourself learning.

3. Swap your tea to herbal or matcha tea, or swap your coffee to tea … or vice versa.

4. Change hands when using the computer mouse for a month.

5. Reverse your car into your garage or park somewhere different from your normal parking spot.

6. Wear the other two-thirds of your closet. Or better yet, just give them away to charity.

7. If you have a regular eating spot at work, try somewhere completely different this month.

8. Instead of checking your social media every day for this month, check it once a week and call your friends more.

9. Watch your "ums" or "ahs" for a month (if you are serious here, join an organization like Toastmasters).

10. Monitor yourself for complaints. Stop and watch how many times you complain per day (a great website here is a complaintfreeworld.org).

<u>DAY 3: THE POWER OF OTHERS</u>

"Don't worry about people stealing your ideas. If your ideas are any good, you'll have to ram them down people's throats."

- Howard Aiken Physicist

Beginning a new venture alone can be hard. Beginning it with others, however, can often be harder.

If you are 'flying solo', success will work best with feedback or support. If you're tempted to go into business with others, consider it like a marriage. You will obviously want to be absolutely sure that they are 'marriage' material. What may seem fun to begin with, may turn out to be a very costly mistake in the long run.

Whatever you decide to do, turning to your friends, relatives, and colleagues for targeted advice will save you time, money, and effort. Just like you wouldn't take financial advice from your barber, don't ask for advice if that's not their area of expertise.

Also, if you know you won't receive support about your ideas from a friend or family, simply don't ask them or let them know. That's why it's so important to surround yourself with people who are not just supportive of you, but who also understand what you are aiming to accomplish.

*Sure, your friends and family might think you're crazy... b*ut they probably think that anyway. Share your idea with a few friends or family members that you trust and see if they have any thoughts on how to develop or enhance your idea.

But what if I have no supportive close friends? The first thing you should do is reach out further than your close friends to your existing peer group and colleagues who you know will be supportive and honest. This will help you develop your idea further. You've already built relationships with these people, so don't leave them by the wayside. They can each offer a unique perspective and opinion on how to improve your idea. Treat this as a small test group for you to see how your idea sits in the marketplace. Keep in mind though that these are only opinions, and we all have our own prejudices and opinions that we bring to the table.

The next step is networking. This may sound counter-intuitive to start networking without a fully-fledged idea, but networking first has major benefits. First, you have access to many more different and diverse opinions and when you are ready for the market, you have already established trust and credibility, making people more comfortable to purchase.

If you're just starting out, you may feel as though you're not ready to interact with these people because you 'haven't proved yourself yet'. This is simply you listening to your own limiting logic. Instead, put yourself out there and start meeting people who are in the same field that you want to build your start-up in. If you don't have the time to attend these meetups, there are plenty of online communities that are equally helpful. Find a community connected to your idea or go to mentoring sites such as score.org and reach out on social media sites like LinkedIn, Twitter, or Facebook to people who you think could be of help.

The Internet is a wealth of resources for those wanting to discover new people. Forums are by far one of the best places you can look. If you're young, it can be more difficult to surround yourself with successful people in real life so be sure to check out local young entrepreneur groups as well as more established business networks. In my experience, forums are helpful. But remember, due to the weakness of connections between anonymous users, forums are not infallible.

For a more hands-on approach in the real world, join start-up co-working spaces, go to entrepreneurial events and meetings in your field, and just start seeking out strangers who you know could help.

If you know your immediate peer group wouldn't support these endeavours, consider temporarily (or permanently) expanding your peer group. Rather than simply hanging out with the same group of friends, try going out with completely new groups of people in social capacities. It might be a little uncomfortable but it can really spark some great friendships (this is particularly useful if combined with networking).

Just be mindful of the two biggest risks faced when sharing ideas.

The first is your negativity.

While you might know your idea is fantastic, other people in your life might not be as onboard as you are. Take feedback as constructive criticism and work on it. It has created the backbone of many businesses, so utilise it.

The second is theft.

A lot of people use this excuse for why they haven't done anything about their idea or even shared it. Most people are honest and the ones who aren't, probably don't have the inclination to apply action on an idea in motion. It's also worth remembering the '100th Monkey' theory. The chances are that somewhere, someone has exactly the same idea as you. If you search and find that others do, don't get disheartened. Find ways to improve on their idea to be different and to create your own unique service proposition, or consider joining forces.

It is vital to have supportive people around you. So don't ignore this.

But what do I talk about? If you are just getting started, you will probably want to listen, more than anything else, especially if the person you're talking to has more experience than you do.

Don't be shy about throwing your ideas around. Again, always consider that a handful of people in the world may already have the same idea. Additionally, these people may have their own businesses, agendas, and ideas they're sitting on. It's better to take the time to get to know individuals and then talk about your idea. This kind of feedback is much more valuable and will lead to better 'connections' for you.

Another option to consider is online surveys. You don't have to eat your own words to see if your idea is worth following. One thing you can do is implement a voting system for your idea. You can have people vote from forums (using a service like Survey Monkey) or set up a survey and get some of your social media contacts to vote. If you have a few dollars to spend, you could try testing it through Google Adwords (for more information on this, Google it!).

These three options are very easy to set up even if you are a computer novice.

ACTION STEPS

Get out of your comfort zone and start meeting new people who want to build businesses (or who already have). You never know where these connections can take you. Try to meet at least one new unique individual each week.

DAY 4: UNDERSTAND YOUR REASONS FOR WHY YOU NEED TO DEVELOP YOUR IDEA

"The brain is a wonderful organ; it starts working the moment you get up in the morning, and does not stop until you get into the office."

- Robert Frost, Poet

Whenever you are launching a business venture, you need to know why you're doing it. For many people it is about money – we take risks and launch businesses because we want a financial reward at the end of the day. But you need to get to the root of *why* you want the money. Take time. Set an amount. Set a date. Get specific and get your reasons on paper. Better yet, try a freemium software like Evernote or Trello and get your objectives written.

There are, of course, other reasons for starting a business. Maybe you just dislike working for other people or perhaps you want to do something that really helps others in your community... whatever your reason, remember it and use it.

Why do you need to identify this?

This is your source of motivation. It is your mojo, your long-term fuel, your reasons for ownership. It is important to note that all lasting motivations are internal; you need to have the inner drive to push forward even when things are difficult. Don't seek external motivation from outside sources because at the end of the day, it is only temporary. Internal motivation is your lifeblood. Find it. Leverage it.

Things will get difficult.

Seth Godin wrote a book called "The Dip"_and in it, he presents a simple idea: Getting any idea up and running to the point of success is difficult. You'll struggle in the beginning but if you apply yourself intelligently, you will start to see some success. Eventually, however, this success will taper off and you'll enter a crisis point: *the dip*.

Whenever you're considering the launch of an idea, you need to think about not just how hard it will be to get things up and running, but also the dip itself (and in truth you'll encounter multiple dips along the way!). When things are difficult, you need the motivation to stick with it. If you find yourself procrastinating, go back and work on gaining leverage.

Motivation is important. If you're not willing to see the idea all the way to the end, then you should quit right now. Peter Shallard, a psychologist specialising in entrepreneurship, wrote a great article that explains why quitting is sometimes the best option. You don't want to end up like the guy in the article who burns all his bridges, including his friendships while trying to get his business going. You want to know you're passionate to your core about solving a burning issue, as that will help with fulfillment.

We don't have motivation all the time.

Motivation rises and falls over time. No matter how excited you feel about your idea right now, you're going to find motivation lacking in the future (that's part of the dip).

The ebb and flow of your motivation levels are normal and natural. What counts is you stick with it, and through it, if you know you're doing the right thing.

ACTION STEPS

Grab a pen and paper and write down your purpose for building your business. Be honest with yourself. If you are struggling, is this goal worth chasing? What is your plan going to be when things start getting difficult? Make no mistake about it; it's not a question of if things are going to be difficult, but when and how difficult, which is why you need to consider contingency plans to prepare for it as best as you can.

Motivational speaker Anthony Robbins advocates that decision making should be seen in terms of avoiding pain and encouraging pleasure. When you focus on your overarching reason, make sure it's something that gives you intense pleasure (and ideally little pain).

Now, I know I said only 5 minutes each day … but if you can find the time, there is a Ted talk delivered by Anthony Robbins I strongly recommend watching. Whether you love him, hate him, or haven't heard of him, this is by far one of the best TED talks ever given (just look at the reviews) and it is a good external motivational tool. See resource section for details.

P.S. Seth's book "The Dip" short and concise and worth the read. His blog is also one of the most read blogs on the Internet, so check it out as well.

DAY 5: IS YOUR IDEA COMMERCIALLY VIABLE?

"Business is not about money. It's about making dreams come true for others and for yourself."

– Derek Sivers, Entrepreneur

Determining whether your business idea is commercially viable is an art unto itself. You must ask yourself if someone is really willing to spend their cold hard-earned money on your product or service.

Here are some tips to help you answer this question:

1. Make sure that you are removing a strong pain point or are solving some real problems that people have.

2. Make sure you are increasing pleasure for your target market.

3. Know the answers to these questions: Who are your competitors? Is there room in the market for your company? How will you successfully compete with them?

4. Be sure to talk about your idea with other people who would be potential customers and encourage their feedback.

5. If you have an existing business or position that's related to what you want to do, show your idea to current customers.

The most important factor of all.

You absolutely need to be able to map out an accurate financial projection of your company that leads to a profitable ending. If you cannot do this, you are doomed before you even begin.

Take the time to write down your costs for everything from procurement and labour. You need to figure out how much inventory to purchase as to be sure to buy just the right amount. Sum up all your costs. That's how much you're going to need to get everything up and running. If you've never done something like this before, it is worth looking up the terms 'fixed' and 'variable' cost.

Then factor in your revenue. No matter what your guess is for revenue, experience says you should adjust things down by at least 50%. Keep a pessimistic, realistic, and optimistic projected monthly cash-flow of the next 12 months. Monthly cash-flow is how much money is left in the bank at the end of each month. Aim for the optimistic, but be content if you only reach your pessimistic figures.

As long as you see a positive uptick that brings you to profitability in an acceptable amount of time, then you're on the right path!

Build a system and not a job.

Here's the most important thing you need to know about building a business: you must build a system, not a job.

A job is something you work in and it keeps you focused at the micro level. A system is something you work on and allows you to scale to a level greatly beyond your personal capacity.

Imagine for a moment that you own a consulting company. It's a small business, just you. You are responsible for the sales, marketing, finance, and of course, consulting. This is a job, and not just a normal job – it's going to take you 10+ hours a day to get everything done.

Pretend you did one thing differently: hired (or contracted) employees to do parts of the business that are not your area of expertise. Now you are simply responsible for, say, the consulting; something you can easily accomplish in 40 hours a week. You then have time to see the larger picture of where you want to take it.

Suddenly, you are less stressed and, most importantly, you have a system in place that uses your personal competitive advantage. Every new job you get from your sales efforts gets pushed to your workforce. If you excel at marketing, get someone else to help with finances (or vice versa).

When you have too much work, simply hire, outsource assistance, increase your rates or any other number of possibilities and the whole system grows. Thanks to technology, help can cost a lot less that you may think. Having someone do your books for five hours a week may be the difference between your idea surviving or thriving.

Sure, your margins may be slightly lower, but because you can scale, your income potential can be exponentially higher. You've then proceeded to specialise and at the end of the day, you'll be more content that things are moving in the right direction.

ACTION STEPS

If you haven't taken the time to map out cost projections yet, get it done. This is something that is beyond important. You can't go blindly into the woods.

Eventually, you'll stumble and hit things that you could have easily avoided.

Here's a basic finance 101 lesson: Figure out your costs and potential revenue, and then subtract the two to get your profit. If things look low, that's okay. What you are looking for is the increase in profit as time goes on.

Additionally, be sure to arrange your business so that it is a system and can be scaled. This can't be emphasized enough. The most important thing is to (at some point) be able to remove yourself from the equation. There are many excellent resources on validating your product and I would recommend you read an article called 'your first 1000 true fans' by Kevin Kelly (see resources section for link).

DAY 6: DEVELOP AN INTERNET PRESENCE

"Give a person a fish and you feed them for a day; teach that person to use the Internet and they won't bother you for weeks."

– Unknown

You can't deny that the Internet has been responsible for many success stories.

Even Justin Bieber found his way to success through the Internet.

If you want an Internet presence (and there are few reasons why you wouldn't), here's eight simple action steps that you need to do without the fluff and fillers.

STEP ONE: PURCHASE A DOMAIN AND WEB HOSTING.

You want a domain that is short, memorable and reflects what your business is offering. Generally, a 'dot com' address is more powerful than any other extensions. If your target market is in your country, buy your country domain listing as well. Domains are only a few dollars, so if you want, you can get both your country and the 'dot com' addresses. Most Internet entrepreneurs recommend hostgator.com, dreamhost.com or crazydomains.com to purchase your domain. When you buy the domain, you'll also need hosting so you can upload your site. Just remember when you're purchasing your domain (and web hosting); not to succumb to all the bells and whistles they will add on. It's not worth your money yet. Total cost here should be under $100.

STEP TWO: BUILD A QUALITY WEBSITE.

So long as you are not trying to make the next Facebook, the best thing to do is get a WordPress site designed. One of the best ways is to buy a template from sites such as Theme Forest. If you're on the smallest of budgets search for free WordPress themes. If you have a few $100 to play with, consider getting one custom built through upwork.com, freelancer.com or 99designs.com. These are outsourcing sites with thousands of employees waiting for projects from around the world. As the cost of living and income varies around the world, you can generally get affordable and quality work produced by virtual employees.

Once you've found your theme, I would recommend either getting one of these outsourcing sites to then upload the WordPress theme you want onto your site. You can do this yourself, but for a cost of under $100 in most cases, it will save you watching a lot of YouTube videos on how to do this yourself.

Upwork.com, formally known as odesk.com, also enables you to 'track' your employees' and they have better searching tools. All sites do the same job, so find out what suits your needs best.

Using these sites is as easy as 'posting a job', and potential workers will show up bidding at your 'online' doorstep. When posting a job, be sure to hire people based on their level of English proficiency, previous client satisfaction, pay rate, and expertise. If you have a higher budget and want something unique, consider searching around your city or looking at websites you like (the site designer will often be credited at the bottom of the site). Otherwise, outsourcing is your best option.

STEP THREE: GET YOURSELF A LOGO.

Your website will need a logo. There are so many designers and design competition sites to choose from. There are three design competition websites I would personally recommend looking at. These are 99designs.com, designcrowd.com, and 48hourslogo.com. I've used my fair share of these sites over the years, but if you are after a quick and cheap logo, try 48hourslogo.com. I originally used this one because they had the lowest minimum design competition cost ($99 at last check). It has thousands of designers who will submit designs for your logo (including mine!).

STEP FOUR: BUILD CONTENT.

Begin by writing about your idea, product or service. If you don't like writing, again, you can outsource writers on any of the above outsourcing websites. There are also writing specific websites such as epicwrite.com. Your site needs interesting content, otherwise visitors to your site will leave uninterested. Also, remember that if your site or idea needs something that doesn't concern writing, you can find engineers, developers, and all sorts of specialities on outsourcing sites. If you are after an expert for creating credibility, there is a site called guru.com, that is, well, full of gurus!

STEP FIVE: SPREAD THE WORD; GET AN AUTORESPONDER.

An autoresponder is your tool to spread the word. If people come to your site, chances are they are interested in your idea. The best way to help them and to spread your word is to grab their email address. This is where an autoresponder helps you and them as well: it allows visitors to enter their email address, which lets them get updates from your site.

This also builds you a powerful list of qualified potential 'clients' for when you think you may have a product they like. The two best options are Mailchimp.com and Aweber.com. Mailchimp is great if you are on a tight budget as they have a free offer up to a certain number of email addresses. It's also considered more user-friendly, but this is a personal preference. However, if you are able to spend a bit of money (last check it was only around $174 a year), then I personally like Aweber because of its tracking, features, and usability. However, the services they offer are similar. One company of mine is using Aweber whilst another is using Mailchimp. Don't get bogged down in which one to choose.

STEP SIX: MONETIZING YOUR IDEA.

Now that your product or service is your main focus, make sure you set up your site so that it clearly illustrates your unique service positioning and competitive advantage, and why people should buy from you. If you need a payment tool for your site, get your developer to set it up. If you're just starting out, then PayPal is likely to be the best choice for you. Long-term, consider payment options like Stripe.com, braintree.com or Eway.com

This is a decision best left to you and your developer. Research is key.

STEP SEVEN: MONETIZING OTHER PARTS OF YOUR SITE.

Until you have your own product developed and up for business, there are a few other options you could consider earning more money on your website. Here are three of the easiest:

1) Sign up for a Google AdSense account.

Advertising is most easily accomplished with Google's AdSense program. The person you hire to design your site will be able to easily implement these ads on your site. You won't make much money with AdSense (the joke is, it's called ad 'cents' for a reason!), until you have decent traffic but you will earn a few cents here and there, which can help.

2) Sign up to the Amazon Affiliate Program.

If you are passionate about books and find yourself recommending books a lot, this is a potential side revenue stream. It pays very little (initially about 4-6% of the revenue of each sale), but is worth using while you get yourself up and running. An important point here is that the % is on any item that person buys on Amazon after they clicked on your affiliate link- not just the item.

3) Sell affiliate products.

Sites like Clickbank and Commission Junction are loaded with products that may relate to your idea. Let's say your business is offering Yogilates courses in your city (a mix between Yoga and Pilates). You may find on these sites a Yogilates home course program you try and really like.

You then can start promoting it on your website and share the revenue. Typically, revenue share is between 40% and 70%, which means that a $40 product will net you around $20. Not too shabby for a little bit of effort (and keep in mind, that "little effort" can be outsourced).

Of course, these three options won't generate substantial income, at first, but they are relatively passive once set up so you can then focus on what matters, your main product or service. To get this to happen, however, you need traffic to your website.

STEP EIGHT: GET TRAFFIC TO YOUR WEBSITE.

Here are three common strategies:

1. Use an advertising service.

You can use something like Google Adwords. This is the opposite side to Google Adsense.

Those ads you see delivered by Google were created in Adwords. Before you start with Adwords, make sure your product is clearly ready for sale on your website. Otherwise, you are sending people to your site and the only way you'll make money is through advertisements and affiliates. The math doesn't work out! (You would be trading dollars for cents).

You also need to learn some of the basics about keywords and the AdWords ecosystem in order to make great use of it. If you are a newbie, sign up for an AdWords account and check out their Keyword planner tool. This is the best way to validate your assumptions on a product as it shows you exactly how many people are searching for a particular keyword each month.

2. Writing more articles.

You can outsource them or write them yourself. The purpose of articles is to place them on the web outside of your website. Go to websites that are in your same niche or would want to potentially purchase your product, and ask if they will post your article on their site along with a link back to your own. This helps your site rank in search engines and is called 'guest posting'. Get yourself on several different websites and spread the word of your brand.

3. Go rogue.

Talk to everyone you know and send emails to people you haven't talked to in a long time who may be interested.

Mention your passion for the new business idea and ask if they would suggest it to others who may be interested. Use social media and spend no more than 10 minutes a day on it. Be sure to print yourself business cards, but don't design them yourself. You can get someone else to design a quality card for around $20 to $50 online. The person who designed your logo can do it or simply hire someone else. There are many online printing cards that will print your cards cheaply. But there are three irrefutable laws of ordering cards: (1) Just like booking a flight online: you don't need to succumb to all the extras; (2) Get quality card thickness (350-420mm is great). It shows professionalism, and (3) Go for double sides for maximum benefit (How many newspapers are only one sided?!).

These eight steps are a great overview of how to get your web presence up and running without the fillers. If you have any further questions, a quick google search will reveal plenty of guides and tutorials. The trick doesn't go for information overload and just get started. The minimum cost for all of these steps can be as little as $200.

P.S. If you want your business idea to be location independent, you'll need to be building a business online from the start and will have to master an arsenal of skills to make this a reality. To get these skills takes time and to narrow the time, takes the right learning. Know your objective at the beginning and find others in your field that you want to emulate. It will be worth it in the end.

DAY 7: KEEP YOURSELF MOTIVATED

"If a man does not know to what port he is steering, no wind is favourable to him."

– Seneca, Philosopher

Welcome to D-Day.

This is our final day together and before we both get sentimental, let's work on what you need to stay disciplined. By now you should know exactly what port you are sailing towards, and the wind should be working favourable with you. Still, as addressed in day five, there are going to be times when your motivation falters.

Business rewards persistence. Those who dip their little toe in the water for fear of getting cold aren't going to get anywhere dabbling with their business ideas. If you want to be successful, you'll have to dive in – and stay in.

Copyblogger is one of the most respected blogs on the web, but if you check out their site, it doesn't look much like a blog. Over the last decade, they've evolved to their current form – but it all started with two articles a week written by a single man. For the first three months, the site saw no traffic, and then it began gaining traction. If you think that took patience, it wasn't until a year and a half later when Copyblogger finally made any money. Then 'overnight' it exploded into a highly successful business after it launched its first product. Today, Copyblogger easily earns millions per annum.

Many great ideas fail just before the seed is about to sprout and this is often due to discipline. Copyblogger exists precisely because of its tenacity.

Lifelong Learning.

Learn terms like MVP, SEO or SEM. You aren't aiming at being a pro, but familiarise yourself with any other number of essential skills a savvy business owner needs to have in his or her toolbox. Learn to maximise your time. Try to listen to a podcast or audio book while walking or driving.

The reason most businesses fail is simple: they do not get enough customers. Their product/service offering is typically where it needs to be, but sales are the problem. Learning effective and efficient marketing is one of the most important things you can possibly do, and it's highly recommended. Get creative. Go guerrilla style. Use your imagination. Many of the most memorable campaigns weren't the most expensive.

What if I fail?

That's the beauty of the modern business landscape. As long as you don't take out a gigantic loan or mortgage your children, you get all of the potential upsides with none of the negatives.

So what if your business fails? Most successful entrepreneurs have a few unsuccessful businesses under their belts. Think of it as a 'coming of age' story. Because in truth, you are then just one failure closer to your ultimate success.

And if you do hit the jackpot off the bat, well that's all the better. If you approach this with a great strategy and a fantastic idea, you're closer to the 10% who are likely to be successful. Plus, with the low start-up costs in technology getting smaller, your success is much higher than without it.

Remember at the end of the day the reasons why you are doing this. Those reasons have a lot to deal with freedom and fulfilment. It will be worth it if you can go out there any apply yourself.

Let's close the last day with a story from the late Jim Rohn.

Jim Rohn grew up little more than an average farm boy. He went to college but dropped out, and at age 25 he found himself working as a stock clerk for Sears and with no money in the bank.

He felt discontent; he had a lot of ambition but didn't see any way to realise his dream. With the help of a mentor and some new like-minded friends, Jim became a millionaire through business at age 31 ...

Only to lose it a few years later when his company went bankrupt.

Jim didn't call it quits there, though. He rebuilt from scratch until he once more had the money and lifestyle he wanted. He built multiple businesses, became a public speaker, wrote 17 different books and audio/video programs, and led a very successful life. Not bad for a farm boy from Idaho.

He got there from hard work and persistence. It is that simple. Just start clocking your time into your idea. Sometimes you have to live a few years like others won't, so you can live the rest of your life like others can't.

I hope you have learnt something out of these seven days and it was worth your time and attention. If you need any help, or would like to share feedback, a story, suggestions or an idea, please send me an email as I would love to hear from you. Good luck in taking the next steps with your idea.

RESOURCE LIST

"Don't let your learning lead to knowledge. Let your learning lead to action."

– Jim Rohn

For a full list of resources with clickable links, go to JetEllison.com/resources.

Books and Articles:

Getting Things Done (2015), David Allen

The $100 Startup (2012), Chris Guillebeau

59 Seconds (2009), Richard Wiseman

The Dip (2008), Seth Godin

Kevin Kelly, 1000 True Fans:

kk.org/thetechnium/1000-true-fans/

Tony Robbins Ted Talk:

www.ted.com/speakers/tony_robbins

Princeton Study on Multi-tasking:

www.ncbi.nlm.nih.gov/pubmed/21228167

Website Resources:

www.trello.com

www.evernote.com

www.todoist.com

www.complaintfreeworld.org

www.Toastmasters.org

www.Meetup.com

www.Score.org

www.Surkeymonkey.com

www.upwork.com

www.freelancer.com

www.99designs.com

www.wordpress.com

www.themeforest.com

www.48hourslogo.com

www.designcrowd.com

www.epicwrite.com

www.guru.com

www.aweber.com

www.mailchimp.com

www.stripe.com

www.braintree.com

www.eway.com

www.adwords.com

www.clickbank.com

www.cj.com

www.copyblogger.com

www.dreahost.com

www.hostgator.com

OTHER BOOKS BY JET ELLISON

Excerpt from "Trello and GTD Mastery" book:

Like most productivity hackers and entrepreneurs, I have used everything. There are hundreds of products out there to organise your professional and personal life, so why use the Getting Things Done ("GTD") methodology with Trello?

First, let's answer the why behind GTD. The reason here is it is simple enough that you won't get bogged down in the details. If used properly, it will enable you to systemize your life, and work through the cloud of information in your brain. More importantly, it is based on evergreen principles. This means the GTD principles are to a large extent, timeless. GTD has been around since 2001, yet the systems in play have been around much longer than that.

The best resource for this is undoubtedly the principles outlined in David Allen's, "GTD" book. If you have not read it, you will learn the fundamentals in the next chapter, however, I strongly urge you to immerse yourself in the process. It will do wonders for your organisational psyche.

Second, why Trello? Put simply, it works. It is easy to use, yet comprehensive enough to run the majority of start-ups. It is flexible, allowing you to use the platform to run your life, company and everything else with one login. It is big enough that you don't need to worry about it crashing or becoming defunct anytime soon. The visual nature of Trello also makes it easy for anyone to interpret, whether that 'anyone' is a new Trello user or team member.

With these two 'powers' combined, you will create one of the finest systems to revamp your personal and professional life.

For more information on Trello GTD Mastery, search Jet Ellison on Amazon.

DON'T FORGET YOUR COMPLIMENTARY BOOKS!

Thank you for reading this book.

To make sure you get the most value out of your journey, here are three exclusive resources that will help you on your entrepreneurial quest.

1. "100 Ways to Gain More Time, Money and Happiness".

We compiled 100 ways to help spark more ideas on how to gain more money, time, and happiness. It is a must read companion with this book.

2. "45 Ways to Increase Productivity for the Entrepreneur"

This gives you 45 amazing ways to get yourself motivated to achieve greater levels as an entrepreneur or employee. Give it a quick read and apply it to your life.

3. "100 Amazing Tips to be a More Successful Entrepreneur"

This short book gives you 100 tips and tactics on becoming a better entrepreneur. Print it out and keep it by your side when you are in need of motivation.

You can download these three incredible resources here for free:

www.jetellison.com/amazongifts

Any questions, please don't hesitate to contact me at www.jetellison.com. If you'd like to connect with me on Twitter, follow @ellison_jet.

With gratitude,

Jet Ellison

THANKS FOR READING. NOW, WHAT?

Dear Reader,

Before you go, sincere thanks for reading this book. I hope you received as much value from it as I did in writing it. If you enjoyed this book, I would love an honest review since the success of this book relies largely on favourable Amazon reviews.

I would love to hear valuable feedback and helpful comments as this will help with future updates. If you have any personal stories you would like to share, please feel free to email me through the website www.jetellison.com.

With gratitude,

Jet Ellison

www.ingramcontent.com/pod-product-compliance
Lightning Source LLC
Chambersburg PA
CBHW021414170526
45164CB00002B/645